– VOLUME 1 –

TASTE ISLAND LIFE

All holidays
are whole small lives
lived somewhere else...

With contributions by Alexander McCall Smith,
Ellen Himelfarb, Kathleen Jamie, Liz Lochhead,
Sir Bernard Crick and Charles MacLean

Published by Isle of Jura Distillery in association with Scottish Book Trust

Isle of Jura Distillery
Craighouse
Isle of Jura
Argyll PA60 7XT
www.isleofjura.com

Scottish Book Trust
Sandeman House
Trunk's Close
55 High Street
Edinburgh EH1 1SR
Tel: 0131 524 0160
www.scottishbooktrust.com

ISBN – 10: 1-901077-20-9
ISBN – 13: 978-1-901077-20-9

Printed and bound in Great Britain by CPI
Typeset and Designed by Adam Nice and Martin Disley
Edited by Marc Lambert

Further copies may be obtained from Scottish Book Trust.

The Isle of Jura Writer Retreat programme is sponsored by Isle of Jura with additional
support from the Scottish Executive and Arts & Business New Arts Sponsorship Awards.

Scottish Executive
New Arts Sponsorship Awards
In conjunction with

Arts & Business Scotland

– CONTENTS –

– THE MUSIC OF AN ISLAND –

BY ALEXANDER McCALL SMITH

THERE IS A certain pleasure in going to a place which takes some time to reach. Most places in Britain can be reached very easily, and quickly, with the result that there is no great sense of making a journey; it is just too easy.

MANY ISLANDS, HOWEVER, still require a journey by sea, and this reminds us that we are going somewhere, leaving something behind. Jura takes a little time to get to, and at least one journey across salt water. When you reach its shores, with the bare hills rising sharply above the road from the ferry, you know that you have crossed over not just a strait but a subtle, invisible boundary. Something is different here.

YOU ARE STRUCK by the emptiness. Islay, the neighbouring island across which one travels to get to Jura, is a gentle place of meadows, farms, distilleries; and then Jura rears up. Here the land is harder, more vertical; there are cliffs, there are clusters of trees clinging to the hillsides, up into the mists. There are signs of a human hand on the landscape, but they are few, and many of them come from a long time ago — the foundations of old crofts, a few stones, lichen-covered, fences of old iron posts and wire that is red with ancient rust. The modern world in which most of us are obliged to live has

a cluttered, over-used texture, the very air we breathe feeling second, third-hand. It is different here. This is on the edge of a country, a continent. This is fresh, unsullied; there is a purity in this place.

BUT EVEN IF Jura has a tiny population — less than two hundred people — it is not a lonely place. Craighouse is the perfect size of village for the stranger to feel at home. There is a focus: the pier and the tiny harbour, the shop, the hotel and its lively bar, the distillery with its bustling yard. Perhaps there is everything here that one needs to be content. Certainly there is the friendliness that one associates with such places — the courteous greetings, the polite, but shy, interest in the business of others, the sense that one does not have to live life at breakneck speed. My stay coincided with two major island events: the sports at Ardlussa House, an isolated, romantic deer-stalking estate further up the island, and the sports ceilidh in the village hall at Craighouse. The whole island was at both occasions. At the sports, in spite of a deluge of rain, we stood and watched while the man who had won the shotput for the last decade, a mighty shepherd clad in estate tweeds, won his event yet again, while in another part of the field, rain-bedraggled children wriggled their way through the obstacle course. These are small, local things, but they make up a life that is both good and rooted, and seeing them makes one realise how much those of us who live in cities are missing.

AT THE CEILIDH in the evening those who had been drenched at the sports arrived dried and changed and ready to dance. The children were there, from four or so upwards, and even teenagers, who elsewhere seem to be so apart from everything, were dancing a Strip the Willow and the rest, and knew the steps. Obviously the island school still teaches them these things when they are younger, and they remember. The music was provided by a single musician, a Jura man who played the accordion, and played it well. He never falters, they told me. He never misses a note.

THIS IS A place to inspire. Being part of a community like this, even for a short time, experiencing the warmth of its welcome, sensing the very real peace and resolution that lies at its heart — these have an effect on the soul. Christopher Grieve — the poet Hugh MacDiarmid — said something in one of his poems about the contentment that comes from hearing the music of our Scottish islands. He meant music in the broadest sense — the music of the wind-swept landscapes, the music of the sea against the rocks, the music of the burns in spate, the music of an entire culture. That music is still there on Jura, beguiling, heart-breaking, particular to place.

3

– EVANS WALK –

BY KATHLEEN JAMIE

i Atlantic to Atlantic, ocean to ocean
the path climbs
up through lush grasses

Cloudless sky. Moor silent
but for fly-buzz.
Relief of the Abhainn Bheag
splashing over pebbles.

ii In its sliver of shade
I rest, conversing
with a huge erratic boulder

about raised beaches,
glaciers, the last ice-age...
It is slow to answer.

iii The path guides me
up over moor to the watershed,
where begins a chain of four lochans.
Then a westward flowing river.

The Paps are forbidding high
bare scree. But ahead, a V

-shaped notch in the land
reveals blue Atlantic, distant isle of Colonsay.

iv Waterfalls, and a slog
across a plain of head-high
boggy, fly-ridden bracken.
Just one warbler singing.

v On the white, empty
sands at Glenbatrick
I collect exquisite
mother-of-pearl shells.

vi The same path back —
up to the pretty lochan
whose surface is flashing
electric-blue: dragonflies.

Watershed again.
In the distance, the mainland —
the blue Sound of Jura
one white sail, passing.

– NO EXCUSES BUT HONESTLY –

BY LIZ LOCHHEAD

hard to draw
Jura's beauty —
foxgloves and fuchsia far too flashy for
just black and white
hard to write —
the mountains with their purple passages
the long curve of empty road
the wide swathe of empty moor
the too-blue-for-Scotland sky
this
intricacy of thistles
far too intent on being emblematic

– A TRULY MAGICAL PLACE –

BY ELLEN HIMELFARB

THERE ARE A few microclimates in Britain where a sub-tropical paradise can invade the evergreen forests and rose gardens typical of the country. The Isle of Wight is one; Scilly is another. That a third can be found on the Hebridean Isle of Jura, which dangles unprotected in the Atlantic Ocean, sounds dubious, but it's true.

JURA HAS THE windswept, desert-of-the-north quality of a place fit only for the propagation of sheep (and make no mistake: there are plenty of sheep here). But there is an oasis of sorts at Jura House Gardens, within three-foot-thick stone walls built nearly 200 years ago.

A GARDEN HAS been here, in some form or other, for generations — ever since the Campbell clan first occupied Jura House, in the late 18th century. Since the 1930s, the mansion has belonged to the Riley-Smith family, which, 30 years ago, hired a soft-spoken Dutchman called Peter Cool to tend its grounds.

THE NAME IS apropos. Cool takes a "things happen" attitude to the garden, preferring wildflowers and artful experimen-

tation to fastidious organisation. "When I was young and deciding what to do with my life," he says, "I had a choice between art and gardening. My brother chose art, so I combined the two." When he first arrived at Jura House, the grounds were a lot wilder, with a few old yew trees, thick boxwood and some of the beech hedges you see today — plus heaps of deep-set bracken that would take seven years to pull. Having been trained in organic gardening he, naturally, cultivated an organic vegetable garden. At the time, however, the profession was unheard of — at least in this corner of the British Isles. "I was thought of as a weirdo by some," says Peter. In a move that seems, in retrospect, to have been remarkably unlucky (considering the big business in organic foods today), he eventually pulled up the veg in favour of something more ornamental and, 20 years ago, began the "trial and error" endeavour that is the garden's present incarnation.

STILL AN ORGANIC guru of sorts around the Western Isles, Peter has nurtured a five-plot show-garden that is 100 per cent organic — a marvel when you consider that many of the plants are non-native, from seeds collected on his travels. His giant ferns, palms and spiky Atherosperma moschatum are Tasmanian; the striking four metre conical echium pininana are from the Canary Islands. "When you use chemicals," he says, "you kill the bugs, yes, but you also kill everything around them. I don't use sprays here. I feed the plants naturally. They get vital energy and are healthy, and because they are healthy they can fight against anything." It must help that the garden benefits from the Gulf Stream, a high level of rainfall and a south-facing slope to the coast. "If this garden were at Kew, it would have to be kept inside," says Peter.

PETER HAS NOTICED the climate slowly changing, and this is mirrored in the plants, which keep their blooms later and later, year upon year. This year, he says, the garden is at its best in early June, when there is fresh growth and the colours are most radiant. ("It is all about colour," says Peter, who used a trial-and-error method of making all the flowers work together.) In summer there are wild poppies in saturated reds, yellows and cornflower blue; dazzling magenta foxglove; rose campion; and daisies to "strike a balance". Great patches of wildflowers flank the path down to the beach: wild geraniums, bluebells and native grasses. And Peter didn't destroy all his organic vegetables back when the new garden was taking shape; he kept giant artichokes, rhubarb, asparagus and wild rocket, which he harvests for the island's 180 residents and the 3,000 visitors who drop by each season.

GUESTS ENTER THROUGH a stone archway, or "moongate", that Peter built from

slate "shingles" he found scattered around the island's forests, roads and quarries. "Jura is one of the only places where you can just use things lying around." The inspiration for his design was a similar structure by landscape artist Andy Goldsworthy that Peter spotted at the Chelsea Flower Show. But where Goldsworthy famously uses only dry stone in his moongates, Peter had to make a concession with his, adding cement to hold the stones in place. The arch is a theme throughout the garden, echoed in crescent-shaped hedge borders and driftwood benches with arched backs that Peter placed at the base of a grassy knoll. The only non-organic embellishments are the heavy rust-coloured metal clam-drudging pots that he found washed up on the seashore, then hauled up to use as a decorative motif.

BUT DON'T TAKE our word for it. Each year, Peter redesigns one of the existing plots to the specifications of his latest whim, so things maybe very different very soon. This year, he has been experimenting with planting in dry, rocky soil. Next year, who can tell? Says Peter: "There is no end to it."

Did we catch too much sun later

in the blaze of the gardens,

among the astonishing arches, barbered slopes

and walled gardens of exuberant exotica?

Was it when I lingered in the shade of the sheds

selecting us each an artichoke for supper,

till, leaving the money in the trustbox,

I came out into the sun again to

see you with Peter Cool the gardener,

who was showing you, cupped in his hand, that

perfect-looking house martin that somehow could not fly?

No, I think we burned up

as we drew by the tea tent,

you and I facing in different directions,

so engrossed in what we were doing

we didn't notice time passing or the sun beating down

or those so cheeky chaffinches sneaking under

the paper napkins to steal our lemon cake...

— FROM CORNUCOPIA BY LIZ LOCHHEAD

– GARDENER'S SHED –

BY KATHLEEN JAMIE

Spiderwebs at the skylight.
Swallow droppings on the earth floor.
A bee meanders through the half open

stable-door. Out in the orchard
apples swell. Raspberries
redden against a stone wall;

roses mixed with drifts
of faded pink geraniums show
through an arch in the beech hedge.

Here rests his spade. A riddle
leans behind a pail. A pair of gloves,
work-weary, hang from a nail.

INVER ESTATE

ARDFIN ESTATE

FOREST ESTATE

TARBERT ESTATE

RUANTALLAIN ESTATE

ARDLUSSA ESTATE

BARNHILL ESTATE

26

– PIER IN THE MORNING –

BY KATHLEEN JAMIE

Rain falls softly, puckering the sea.
The small isles are ghostly in mist.

Moored to an orange buoy
a rusty fishing boat from Ullapool

Bottle-bank, public lavatory, stack of lobster creels.
When will anyone wake?

– CORRAN SANDS –

BY KATHLEEN JAMIE

Between the emergency airfield and the sands
tangle extravagant numbers of wildflowers: foxgloves
wander on maddened journeys toward death,
gorse pods pop in the afternoon heat. Purple grasses,
yellow rattle, eyebright, hawksweed, ragwort, clover,
devil's bit scabious, spires of purple loostrife,
bird's foot trefoil, knapweed, frothy meadowsweet,
(must be a damp bit) orchids, speedwell, dandelion
- and feeding on nettles, a squad of black caterpillars,
speckled silver, like a starry night in winter.

*

Far out on the mile-long strand,
a woman promenades a baby in a pram
with a pink parasol, and an entourage
of five sleek sheepdogs.

UPSTAIRS

POSTCARDS

ELECTRICAL
TOYS

WAX JACKETS
FISHING TACKLE
WELLINGTONS

BOOKS
MAPS
ETC...

NO   UNACCOMPANIE
ALLOWE   UP

45

– EVENING –

BY KATHLEEN JAMIE

Behind the grey Paps the sun sets, tinting the clouds
mauve and powder pink; the sheeny waters of Small
Isles Bay borrow the same colours. On each rock
offshore a seal lolls; one suckling a grey pup.
Silence, but for wavelets lapping the shore, and once:
the weird, shivery cry of a red-throated diver.

– WHISKY DISTILLING ON THE ISLAND OF DEER –

BY CHARLES MACLEAN

I T WOULD BE safe to suppose that whisky distilling has taken place on Jura since time immemorial, although there is no written evidence. I say this because Jura's was a pastoral economy — Highland cattle were the staple items of trade and wealth until the mid-19th century, when sheep came to dominate.

AS HAPPENED ELSEWHERE in the Highlands, "the beasts" were brought indoors during the hard winter months and kept alive with the residues of brewing and distilling, the husks and spent grains, known as "draff". The secrets of distilling had been known on neighbouring Islay since at least the 1490s, and possibly for two centuries before that.

JURA ITSELF IS the wildest island in the Inner Hebrides: a huge area of rock and blanket bog, most of it without roads or habitation of any kind. It was not easy to grow crops on such terrain; some oats were grown, and a dwarf barley called bere, but most were imported from Islay and Kintyre. From early times sparse human habitation clung to the east coast, evidenced today by mysterious megaliths and standing stones. On the west side, a small clachan once existed at Ruantallain, at the mouth of Loch Tarbert, and another at

Glengarrisdale in the north-west corner of the island until it was abandoned in 1947. Here there is a cave which, until about thirty years ago, contained some bones and a skull belonging to a Maclean who was killed when the perfidious Campbells attacked the island in 1647, during the Wars of the Covenant.

AS MORE THAN one writer has observed: "On Jura it is easy to believe that there is no such thing as the human race." Such humans who did live there will have been glad of a drop of whisky!

DISTILLING FOR PRIVATE consumption (i.e. not for sale) was perfectly legal until 1781. After this it was summarily banned — which simply meant that people did it covertly. Jura is famous for its many caves, and it seems likely that such places were used by the "smugglers". Certainly, there is a strong tradition that a cave at Craighouse, close to the site of the present Isle of Jura Distillery, was used for such purpose. In 1810 a rudimentary distillery was erected outside the cave, by the owner of the island, Archibald Campbell. In its early days, this small distillery may have been operated by David Simson, the founder of Bowmore Distillery on Islay, and the true "father" of legal distilling on that island.

CAMPBELL'S NEW BUILDINGS included a maltings to convert barley into malt. The "green malt" itself was dried over locally cut peats, which will have imparted a smoky taste, not unlike that found in such Islay malts as Lagavulin, Ardbeg and Laphroaig. The first licensee we know of is William Abercrombie in 1831, but he only had it a year, handing over to Archibald Fletcher.

"THE SMALL ISLES Distillery", as it was named, would remain in Fletcher hands for 20 years, but they didn't make much of a success of it. They were owing rent by 1835, and by the time they gave up had only 5,450 litres of whisky in bond — and this of doubtful reputation. Campbell's factor tasted some of Fletcher's "best aged whisky" in 1851, and showed it to the manager of Caol Ila Distillery, "...who makes the best whisky on Islay. I could not get him to express himself as to whether Jura could be improved or not, he merely said old or new it retained its former taste..."

THE LAIRD THOUGHT of selling the distilling equipment for scrap: the copper and brass were valued at £400, and the whole plant at £600. The day was saved, however, when he was approached by a Mr. Buchanan from Glasgow, who signed a lease on condition that he be supplied all the peat he needed from the estate, and that local farmers would take up all the draff. In spite of also taking the lease of Caol Ila Distillery, Buchanan went bust within ten years. His successors in the Small Isles Distillery lasted a mere four years.

FEINTS

SPIRIT

SPIRIT & SAMPLE SAFE

IN 1876 A thirty-four year lease was signed between the then laird, James Campbell, and James Fergusson & Sons of Glasgow. The Fergussons invested some £25,000 in improvements to the distillery, increasing capacity to 817,000 litres of spirit per annum, and making it "one of the easiest worked distilleries in the district", according to the indomitable traveller, Alfred Barnard, who visited in 1886. The Fergussons also undertook to build a pier capable of taking vessels of ten-foot draught at low water, and constructing a road, a bridge and a waiting room on the pier head.

BUT RELATIONS BETWEEN them and the laird were not good. There had been some angry exchanges in the mid-1890s, and when James Campbell died in 1901, to be succeeded by his son, the Fergussons quit Jura, taking with them all their new plant and machinery, and gradually removing their stocks of mature whisky. They continued to pay rent until the expiry of the lease in 1918, but Colin Campbell pursued them for repairing the pier — estimated at £1,293, while the Fergussons felt that £67 was closer to the mark! — plus a further £1,000 for dredging the harbour. It is not known whether this dispute was ever settled, but it marked the end of distilling on Jura for many years.

BEFORE WORLD WAR I the population of Jura was over a thousand; by the 1950s it was down to 150 souls. The Second World War had taken its toll, and as with many Hebridean islands, there had been a steady drift of younger people away to the mainland. Ownership was now in the hands of Robin Fletcher (of Ardlussa Estate in the north — no relation to the distilling Fletchers, so far as I am aware), Tony Riley-Smith (of Jura Estate in the south) and three others. As the focal point of a wide ranging plan to increase employment on the island and attract new blood, Fletcher and Riley-Smith determined to rebuild the distillery.

THIS MADE SOUND commercial sense. Demand for Scotch whisky had never been greater. Up and down the land distilleries were being refurbished and expanded, and new ones built. Backing for the project came from Scottish & Newcastle Breweries and the old established blending house, Charles Mackinlay & Company. In 1956 the landowners secured the services of William Delmé-Evans, who had built Tullibardine Distillery at Blackford, near Gleneagles, from scratch between 1947-49.

IN AN INTERVIEW in 2004, shortly before his death, Bill Delmé-Evans recalled: "During 1958 I started designing a new distillery which just about trebled the production capacity of the old one, and by 1963 Jura Distillery was commissioned". He used the same sloping site as the previous distillery, clearing the crumbling remains of the former, except for the manager's house — the tall

building on the right, when viewed from the sea. The water came from the same source as previously — the Market Loch.

"MY PRIMARY AIM was to construct an economic distillery within the space available", he wrote. "Everything had to be simple and fall to hand. You could not afford to complicate things in so remote a location... It was our intention to produce a Highland-type malt differing from the peaty stuff last produced in 1900. I therefore designed stills to give spirit of a Highland character, and we ordered malt which was only lightly peated."

THE FIRST SINGLE malt from the new distillery was released in 1974, but the huge majority of the make went for blending (much of it to Mackinlays). One of the reasons for wanting to produce a "Highland-style" of whisky was that this was more desired by the blenders than the smoky "Islay-style". Of course, the latter is now very popular with whisky drinkers around the world, and in response to this demand, Jura has, since 2002, offered a smoky style called "Superstition".

IN 1976 BILL Delmé-Evans was succeeded as managing director by Dr. Alan Rutherford of the distillery company, with Don Raitt as manager.

THEY IMMEDIATELY SET about replacing the worn-out plant and making improvements in efficiency, as well as expanding the still-house from two to four stills. Capacity was increased to 2.5 million litres of spirit per annum. Dr. Rutherford went on to become Head of Production at United Distillers, emeritus Professor of Distilling at Heriot Watt University and a Lieutenant Colonel in the Parachute Regiment (T.A.).

OWNERSHIP OF JURA Distillery passed to Invergordon Distillers in 1985, then Whyte & Mackay ten years later, when that company was owned by American Brands (later called Jim Beam Brands). In 2001 Whyte & Mackay was bought out by its management for £200 million. John Bulman was manager 1978 until 1985, succeeded by Willie Tait 1985 to 2000, and by Michael Heads 2000 to the present.

SINCE 1995 RICHARD Paterson, Master Blender at Whyte & Mackay, and a legend in the whisky trade, has been responsible for production at the distillery, and for deciding what whiskies to bottle as Isle of Jura single malt.

THE MAKING OF malt whisky is a kind of alchemy, and the way each distillery transmutes the base material (malted barley) into liquid gold is unique to itself, and relies upon tradition and high craft. Bill Delmé-Evans set the style; the men I mention above continue the work, and the skills they employ are little changed from those of the illicit distillers on the Isle of Jura. What a comfort is malt whisky!

With thanks to Richard Paterson, Master Blender, and Michael Heads, Manager, Isle of Jura Distillery.

MAIN REFERENCES:

Neil Wilson, *The Island Whisky Trail* [Neil Wilson Publishing, 2003]

Gavin Smith, *The Whisky Men* [Birlinn, 2005]

Charles MacLean, *Scotch Whisky: A Liquid History* [Cassell, 2003]

Hamish Haswell-Smith, *The Scottish Islands* [Canongate, 1996]

Alfred Barnard, *The Whisky Distilleries of the United Kingdom* [Harper's, 1887]

– JURA AND ME –

BY WILLIE TAIT, ISLE OF JURA MASTER DISTILLER

MY NAME IS Willie Tait and I am the Master Distiller and Brand Ambassador for the Isle of Jura Single Malt Whisky.

THIS POSITION TAKES me all around the world, although I spend most of my time in the USA.

I FIRST WENT to the beautiful Island of Jura in January 1975 with my wife Christine and our son Scott. This new lifestyle was not planned, it was just one of these things that happen to you and changes your life forever. I went there after seeing the job advertised in the paper, though when I applied for the position it did not say where it was, just that it was off the west coast of Scotland. When the MD of the company arrived at our home, to give us an interview, you can guess how taken aback we both were. When he left, we both hurried for a map to see just where this Jura was. I went there as a Tunroom Man and moved on to become a Mash/Still Man. In 1979 I became the Assistant Manager and we all lived in the flats, now known as the lodge. In 1985 I was promoted to Manager, a post I held until late 1999. I was and still am the longest serving Manager of the Jura Distillery. We left the Island after long heartfelt discussions; we think the children still haven't forgiven us. In 2003 the position of Master Distiller and Brand Ambassador for the Isle of Jura was being developed. This was a dream come true for me as now I could tell the world about the whisky we have made and all about this beautiful island. I hope the day will come when you can visit this wonderful island and experience for yourself the Jura inner energy.

AYE, WILLIE

– SOME THINGS I COVET IN JURA LODGE –

BY LIZ LOCHHEAD

that fearsomely fantastical
armchair upstairs made entirely
of antlers and deerhide like
something out of Cocteau's
La Belle et La Bête

the tinpot suit of armour

the little green chipped 1940s
kitchen chairs

the lobster creel for a lampshade

the pink teacup, the typewriter,
the old black phone

the old scuffed leather sofa

the red Paisley throw

the floral lining of the Edwardian
cabin trunk in the Rose Room

the Mozart printed cushions
in the Music Room

that big mad portrait in the
Portrait Room of some little
plumed Lord Fauntleroy
riding on a goat!

the tall French mirror in the
Portrait Room

the huge shell in the White Room
the bluebirds
on the glass fingerplate in the
Bluebird Room

the tipsy wooden seagull
on the bedside table in the
Bluebird Room

the Victorian ladies' hunting jacket

the American Folk Art hangers
with the heart-shaped cut-outs

the tall window in the hall
on the blue wall —
with the perfectly framed
view of one of the Paps

– ORWELL ON JURA –

BY SIR BERNARD CRICK

I ASKED ONE DONALD Darrock, who had once worked the croft at Kinauchdrach near to Barnhill and was later postman and gillie, "Was Eric Blair a friendly man?" On Jura he always went by his real name. "Aye, a friendly man right enough, a kind man, a cup of tea or a dram and the kettle was always boiling."

WELL, TIGHT AND forbidding though Orwell could be, a postman who had come the five miles up the rough track beyond the end of the single-track road could not just be sent away from the doorstep, especially as Orwell's post was sometimes heavy and always included the weekly joint sent from Loch Tarbert on the mainland on Friday mornings and delivered in late afternoon. But Mr Darrock said that Mr Blair didn't like strangers, whether strong hikers or from yachts, just dropping in to see what it was really like at the end of the track on the bleak northern tip. "What did you talk about?" "Oh the kind of things that men talk about over a dram." "Such as?" "Oh I cannot remember — you know, the weather and the prospects (for the season)".

AT FIRST I was inclined to accept that the islanders who had met him only did talk the time of day, so nothing worth

remembering. But a conversation with Angus McKechnie gave me pause. "They say that he didn't get on well with his sister." "Oh I would not know." "A rather forbidding woman they say." "Oh aye, so they do say." "I have heard that he did not welcome his sister descending to look after him and driving his young housekeeper out." "Well now, you know what they say, 'two women in one kitchen'." "A Canadian poet visited him, I forget his name [I didn't] whom she did not like at all and she drove him out, short notice, the middle of an afternoon." "No, Paul Potts you mean, a poor gentleman. It was in the middle of the night. I heard his footsteps on the road to Craighouse." So too late I realised that the islanders had remarkable memories even for small things which could to them on the small island loom large; but they also had a strong protective discretion with strangers (especially a biographer, whom they must have thought of as little better than a journalist or a detective sergeant). They were protective of someone whom, in those days before easy tourism and holiday cottages, the two hundred and fifty inhabitants could regard as almost one of them because he seemed settled on the island and was working a patch of land, however cack-handedly ("not always did he know what he was doing"). However, "he seemed a kindly man and he kept himself to himself and interfered with no one", a great virtue to the islanders, doubtless comparing him with some of the lairds. But they firmly saw him as — two different informants used exactly the same words, as if the judgement had been mulled slowly over pipe and dram — "a peculiar and kindly gentleman." For this bohemian presence was plainly, in social class terms not just evaluatively a gentleman, (as in "real Highland gentleman" said of even a poor man), but a Gentleman indeed.

TOWARDS THE END of the war and amid the unexpected huge success of *Animal Farm*, Orwell had been living in a flat in Canonbury. But he found that sudden fame and too many friends, of very diverse kinds, from drunken poets like Paul Potts to grandees like David Astor, the proprietor and editor of *The Observer*, added up to constant interruptions and distractions. By early 1946 he knew fairly clearly what he wanted to write, what became *Nineteen Eighty-Four* but was nearly called *The Last Man in Europe*. So he told some of his friends that he wanted get right out of London to somewhere, anywhere remote, if possible without a telephone and difficult enough of access from London to deter, certainly in immediate post-war travel conditions, all but the most warmly invited and most resolute friends. David Astor happened to suggest, serendipitously, Jura. The Astors had an estate in the middle of the island and David had often met the laird of the north of Jura, Margaret Fletcher (née Nelson) at her house at Ardlussa where the tarmac road ended twenty-five miles from the hotel at Craighouse where, back then,

the steamers came in. Five miles up the track from Ardlussa was a small house, Barnhill, and two or three miles beyond that were two croft cottages at Kinauchdrach. She had some difficulty finding tenants. Barnhill could hardly pay as a farm. There were two fields, worked from Kinauchdrach, and a vegetable patch, so there was only the illusion — which Orwell embraced, as a past master of doing simple things the hard way — of self-sufficiency in fruit and vegetables. So a writer with, by then, some income was an ideal tenant for Maggie Fletcher. It was pure coincidence that her then husband, who died in 1960, his health destroyed in Japanese prisoner-of-war camps, had been before the war a teacher at Eton where Orwell had, a decade or more before, been an ironic and sardonic scholarship boy.

HE MADE A reconnaissance to Jura for two weeks in September 1945, only moving into Barnhill in May the following year, albeit returning to London in October for the winter and to wind up his affairs in Canonbury. However on 29 December he set off for Jura "to plant fruit trees" he said, but there were travel problems and he did not arrive until late on 1 January. Presumably he was heading for Hogmanay to see, on a new learning curve, the real Scotland; but tragically missed that one night of all nights. The stiff-upper-lipped Englishman made no such admission but the dates speak for themselves even to the most cautious of biographers.

BY AUGUST 1946 Orwell had begun work on *Nineteen Eighty-Four*, tap tapping away on his old portable, usually in his small upstairs bedroom while his sister down below froze out unwanted visitors or kept invited guests at bay until the evening. A particularly unwelcome guest to Avril was Sally McEwan, a former secretary at Tribune where Orwell had been literary editor after leaving the BBC in the last years of the war. For Sally not merely brought a child with her and a cat, who shrieking and wailing fought for territory or chastity all night with the resident tom, but she was a strict vegetarian too. This raised problems in a kitchen whose staples were hare, rabbit, venison, herring and lobster, not to mention the weekly Sunday joint in the post from the mainland. Eric and Avril at least had in common traditional domestic routines. The only thing Sally and Avril found in common was dislike of the free-thinking, monologuing, fantasising Paul Potts. Perhaps together they conspired his expulsion from what to him was his friend's Eden.

REMOTE THOUGH IT was, I had the feeling that some of Orwell's friends or acquaintances took more literally than he really intended that well meant but often not wholly sincere English upper middle class politeness, "Must come up and see my new place sometime, you know." But one set of visitors came whom he really welcomed: his nephew and two nieces, the children of his late sister Marjorie Dakin. Henry Dakin was a second lieutenant in the

army on leave, Jane had just left the Women's Land Army and her teenage sister Lucy was still at school. The happy visit was nearly the end of them all. To make up for neglecting them while in the dogged heat of writing, Uncle Eric proposed an expedition together with his three-year-old adopted son Ricky (Richard) whom he had cared for since the death of his first and true wife, Eileen, back in 1945. They went to the other side of the island in a small boat with an outboard motor and picnicked. Jane and Avril walked back to get on with the hay-making on such a fine day. But on the way back it seems that Eric had misread the tide tables. Instead of skirting the Corryvreckan at ebb tide, one of the fiercest whirlpools in the northern world, they were passing it near to full flood. They got caught in the eddies of one of its many peripheral minor whirlpools. They were tossed about so much that the outboard motor came off its moorings and fell in the sea. Eric, completely calm, suggested that Henry, as the stronger, took the oars. They were pitched onto a small island, but the boat capsized in the water with young Ricky it. The toddler emerged in the arms of an unflappable Eric and they all waited on the rock until they attracted the attention of, as one can usually find in an apparently deserted Hebredian coastline, a solitary lobster fisherman. He got a rope to them across the swell and pulled them one by one into his boat. As they walked back into Barnhill Avril and Jane called out, "What kept you so long?"

THIS NEAR DEATH of the author of *Animal Farm* was worth a garbled paragraph in the Daily Express. One of three phones then on the island must have buzzed through the one switchboard in the post office, manned by one "Effie" who knew everyone's business.

THE PARAGRAPH DID not mention young Ricky, so it sounded vaguely heroic rather than — as some might say — reckless and irresponsible of Orwell. Thinking of Effie, some murmured a tale to me over a glass at a ceilidh in Craighouse, years afterwards. (The ceilidh had erupted when the BBC Arena team, making the 1984 *Life of Orwell* film, had unwisely paid for interviews in cash on the spot). Effie, they said, had suddenly left her post office, married a butcher in Oban and had bought a big, expensive house there. Had she worked out what the Astor's calls from their stockbroker had been about? The islanders were not all unworldly.

SOME VISITORS WERE deterred. He had hoped that Sonia Brownell would visit him, with whom he had had a brief affair in 1945 and who was to marry him in his very last days. But Sonia was Chelsea, silk stockings and jade cigarette holders, not even of the sub-Bloomsbury of the pubs which were the only "clubs" for many of Orwell's ordinary friends. So his travel hints would have been off-putting rather than helpful and enticing. Allow forty-eight hours and bring stout boots, gum boots, oil skins, he said, and to

be sure to bring her food rations as well as a little flour and tea:

I AM AFRAID I am making all this sound very intimidating, but really it's easy enough and the house is quite comfortable. The room you would have is rather small but it looks out on the sea. By the time you get here I hope we'll have got hold of an engine for the boat and if we get decent weather we can go round to the completely uninhabited bays on the west side of the island... At one of them there is a cave where one can shelter and at another a shepherd's hut which is disused but quite livable where one could even picnic for a day or two...

HE HAD BETTER luck with Celia Kirwan, Arthur Koestler's sister-in-law to whom he had proposed but had turned him down gracefully and acceptably with a sincere "but we must remain good friends for ever"; and they did. At least as elegant and as sophisticated as Sonia, she indulged him as well as her curiosity with a visit despite:

DON'T BRING MORE luggage than, say, a rucksack or a haversack, but on the other hand do bring a little flour if you can. We are nearly always short of bread and flour here since the rationing. You don't want many clothes so long as you have a raincoat and stout boots or shoes. Remember the boats sail on Mondays, Wednesdays and Fridays, and you have to leave Glasgow about 8 a.m.

CELIA WITH A rucksack is almost as unimaginable as Sonia in boots.

I THINK HE would have stayed in Jura, with occasional trips to London on publishing business and to see old friends who could not or would not travel, if it had not been for the sudden acceleration of his endemic tuberculosis. He became more and more interested in the life of the crofters, mistakenly but understandably thinking them typically Scottish, rather than a variant of the many diversities of Scottishness. Indeed he went somewhat over the top (or overboard, as it were, plunging into deep whirlpools), in one of the last columns he wrote in Tribune, as ever serious, provocative and comical, but like the great humanist and essayist he was, not always trying to change our minds, more trying to startle us into thought.

UP TO DATE the Scottish Nationalist movement seems to have gone almost unnoticed in England... You have an English or anglicised upper class, and a Scottish working class which speaks with a markedly different accent, or even, part of the time, in a different language. This is a more dangerous kind of class division than any now existing in England. Given favourable circumstances it might develop in an ugly way, and the fact that there was a progressive Labour government in London might not make much difference... I think we should pay more attention to the small

but violent separatist movements which exist within our own island.

"VIOLENT" IS STRANGE, even if deliberately provocative. Perhaps he had been reading too much Hugh MacDiarmid, as untypical, as eccentric but as interesting and stimulating as himself. But he was beginning to think about Scotland as Scotland, not just an address where he could write undisturbed — well, more or less undisturbed.

SOME WRITERS HAVE foolishly thought that Jura was the death of him, and a wee bit deliberate too. This is of a piece with lazy routine Freudian belief that *Nineteen Eighty-Four* is a classic example of "the death wish", rather than the last book the poor man happened to write before he happened to die, already in hospital making notes towards a new and more conventional novel. Two American authors have famously written of his "mad and suicidal sojourn on Jura". I called this isothermic fantasy. Jura is not Aberdeen. The Inner Hebrides lie in the Gulf Stream with a prevailing south-west wind, not the Arctic north-east wind of the east coast.

Frost and snow are rare. Twenty miles down the sound from Jura in Gigha with its Achamore House Gardens is one of the finest azalea, camellia and rhododendron collections in the British Isles.

ORWELL'S POSTHUMOUS REPUTATION has brought many visitors to Jura, at times some say more than is endurable. The owners of Ardlussa rightly try to stop cars going up the track to Barnhill. Too often their tractor and their man had to pull them from the ditch. And the tenants of Barnhill rightly resent casual tourists. Indeed with four full biographies of Orwell — my own, Michael Sheldon's, Gordon Bowker's and D.J. Taylor's - there is nothing new to learn, and Richard Blair has built a new Barnhill across in Ardfern. Nothing really need draw visitors north of the bar in Craighouse where they should drink a dram in his immortal memory. And the old postman told me that the dram Mr Blair gave him was always a double. Where the hell did he get the whisky from in those hard times? In his day there was not even a distillery on the island, let alone such a one as now.

SCOTTISH BOOK TRUST, Scotland's national agency for readers and writers, is delighted to be working with Isle of Jura to create a unique writer retreat programme, based at the beautifully refurbished distillery lodge at Craighouse. The programme will underline Scotland's unique position internationally as a literary and creative nation, with great natural beauty, great local products and some of the most unspoiled and inspiring landscapes on earth. There will be three opportunities per year, focusing on established Scottish, UK and international writers.

JURA IS ONE of the most remote and wild of the Scottish Islands. Famously, it is the place where George Orwell came — in April 1946 — to write 1984, one of the great books of the 20th century and of world literature. He said at the time: "I am anxious to get out of London for my own sake... I want to write another book which is impossible unless I can get six months' quiet..." He needed a place which was "unget-at-able." Visiting Barnhill, the house where he stayed — located in stunning surroundings near the north tip of the island — one can certainly see what he meant, and what lengths he was prepared to go to in order to buffer himself from the outside world. Indeed, the original title for 1984 was *The Last Man in Europe*, a suitable reflection on Jura's geographical situation. A few miles further north along the track is the Corryvreckan whirlpool (lying between Jura and Scarba), one of the world's great natural phenomena, where Orwell nearly lost his life after miscalculating the tidal run. Despite the wild and challenging remoteness, there are strong indications that he intended to make Jura his long-term home. However, in 1949 he was forced to return to mainland Britain due to ill health, dying of tuberculosis in 1950.

NEEDLESS TO SAY, the writers selected will not be expected to endure the privations Orwell faced! But while they will be able to enjoy the luxury of the distillery lodge, they will also be able to taste island life to the full — a place where nature, geography and one of Scotland's finest whiskies come together to make for one of the most wonderful settings on earth.

Marc Lambert, CEO, Scottish Book Trust
www.scottishbooktrust.com

– CURRENT BOTTLING –

BY CHARLES MACLEAN

T HE CHARACTER OF Jura's new make spirit reminds one of pine-sap and gorse flowers, with traces of cinnamon and a hint of ozone — like sea-breeze.

REMEMBER, THE MALT is unpeated, so the whisky is closer to the Highland style than that of Islay, where the "typical" character is pungent, smoky, peaty and medicinal. Jura is an easy, friendly, unchallenging whisky; a classic "island" malt (with maritime notes and salty sea-spray).

THE CASKS IN which the whisky is matured make a huge contribution to mellowing and filling out the original character of the new make.

THE CORE RANGE is bottled at 10, 16 and 21 years old (all at 40% Vol), with Superstition (a mix of 13 and 21 year old malts, at 45% Vol), and "Legacy" (a mix of 10 year old and older whiskies, at 40%, sold only in duty-free outlets).

RICHARD PATERSON, MASTER Blender, has also selected special casks and parcels of casks for limited edition bottling, including the "1984 — George Orwell Edition" (a 19 years old at 42% Vol, from two different kinds of sherry-wood — 800 cases only); 30 years old bottlings from 1973, 1974 and 1975 (all single casks at cask strength in very limited amounts); and a 36 years old from 1965 (which yielded 449 bottles at 44% Vol).

– CONTRIBUTORS –

LIZ LOCHHEAD

Poet and playwright Liz Lochhead has lived in Glasgow since studying painting at Glasgow School of Art. Her first collection of poetry was published in 1972. Her stage plays include: *Blood and Ice*, *Mary Queen of Scots Got Her Head Chopped Off*, *Britannia Rules*, *Good Things*, and *Perfect Days*. Her adaptation of Euripides' *Medea* for Theatre Babel won the Saltire Society Scottish Book of the Year Award in 2001. Babel also produced *Thebans*, her version of the Greek trilogy *Oedipus/Jokasta/Antigone*. She's also done both Molière's *Tartuffe* and *Le Misanthrope* (as Miseryguts) into rude and rhyming Scots. Her poetry collections include *Dreaming Frankenstein*, *Collected Poems*, *The Colour of Black & White* as well as the collection of monologues, lyrics and performance pieces *True Confessions*. She was a recipient of a Cholmondley Award for Poetry, and is a Fellow of Glasgow School of Art and an Honorary Doctor of Letters of Glasgow University. She has been awarded honorary doctorates by the Universities of Aberdeen, Stirling, Strathclyde, Edinburgh, St Andrews, Dundee, Abertay, Queen Margaret University College and Glasgow Caledonian University. She was appointed Glasgow's Poet Laureate in 2005.

KATHLEEN JAMIE

Described in *Poetry Review* as "a poetic voice of international significance", Kathleen Jamie is a part-time lecturer in Creative Writing at the University of St Andrews. She was born in the West of Scotland in 1962, and studied philosophy at Edinburgh. Her books, which include *The Tree House* (Picador, 2004), *Mr and Mrs Scotland are Dead* (Bloodaxe 2002) and *Jizzen* (Picador 1999), have been shortlisted for and won several prestigious literary awards. Her latest poetry collection, *The Tree House* (2004), won Britain's biggest poetry Award — the 2004 Forward Poetry Prize (Best Poetry Collection of the Year) and the 2005 Scottish Arts Council Book of the Year Award. Her book of essays, *Findings* (Sort of Books 2005) won a Scottish Arts Council Book of the Year Award in 2006.

SIR BERNARD CRICK

Sir Bernard Crick was Professor of Politics of Birkbeck College, London and has an honorary degree from the University Glasgow. He was knighted in 2001 for "services to citizenship and political studies". His best known books are *In Defence of Politics* and *George Orwell: a Life* (1980, still in print). He visited Jura several times while writing the biography, then for the BBC Arena *Life of Orwell* film in 1984 and the BBC Scotland film *The Crystal Spirit*. He founded the George Orwell Prize for Political Writing and has lived in Edinburgh since 1984.

CHARLES MACLEAN

Charles MacLean began writing about Scotch whisky 25 years ago, and has published nine books on this subject to date including *Malt Whisky* [Mitchell Beazley, 1997] which has been translated into ten languages, and *Whisky: A Liquid History* [Cassell, 2003], which won Wine & Spirits Book Of the Year 2005 in the James Beard Awards, the most prestigious American gastronomic prize. He was the founding editor of *Whisky Magazine* and is "British Editor" of the Russian glossy *Whisky*. He has been Contributing Editor of the Scotch Malt Whisky Society's Newsletter (where he also chairs the Nosing Panel and writes the tasting notes) since 1995. He is also whisky correspondent for *Scottish Field*, *Scottish Life* (USA) and *SCOTS* (Australia). A member of the Judging Panel (Spirits) of the International Wines & Spirits Competition, and Whisky Consultant to Bonhams Auctioneers, he was elected a Keeper of the Quaich, the industry's highest accolade, in 1992 for "his services to Scotch whisky over many years".

ALEXANDER McCALL SMITH

Alexander McCall Smith has written more than fifty books, including specialist academic titles, short story collections, and a number of immensely popular children's books. But he is best known for his internationally acclaimed *No. 1 Ladies' Detective Agency* series. The first installment, *The No. 1 Ladies' Detective Agency*, received two Booker Judge's Special Recommendations upon its U.K. publication in 1998, and in 2003 received The Saga Wit Award (commonly known as the "silver Booker" for authors over the age of 50). *The No. 1 Ladies' Detective Agency* series now numbers a total of five books (he is working on the sixth) and has been optioned for feature film. The series has become an international bestseller, with more than 10 million copies in print. McCall Smith was born in Zimbabwe (formerly called Southern Rhodesia) and was educated there and in Scotland. He became a law professor in Scotland, and it was in this role that he first returned to Africa to work in Botswana, where he helped to set up a new law school at the University of Botswana. He was Professor of Medical Law at the University of Edinburgh, and has been a visiting professor at a number of other universities, including ones in Italy and the United States. In addition to his university work, he was for four years the vice-chairman of the Human Genetics Commission of the UK, the chairman of the British Medical Journal Ethics Committee, and a member of the International Bioethics Commission of UNESCO.

Special thanks to the photgraphers — Simon Roberts, Andrew Dowsett and Tom Mannion.

- VOLUME 1 -